READING

IN

50

BUILDINGS

STUART HYLTON

AMBERLEY

First published 2016

Amberley Publishing, The Hill, Stroud
Gloucestershire GL5 4EP

www.amberley-books.com

British Library Cataloguing in Publication Data.
A catalogue record for this book is available from the British Library.

ISBN 978 1 4456 5934 3 (print)
ISBN 978 1 4456 5935 0 (ebook)

Typesetting and Origination by Amberley Publishing.
Printed in Great Britain.

Contents

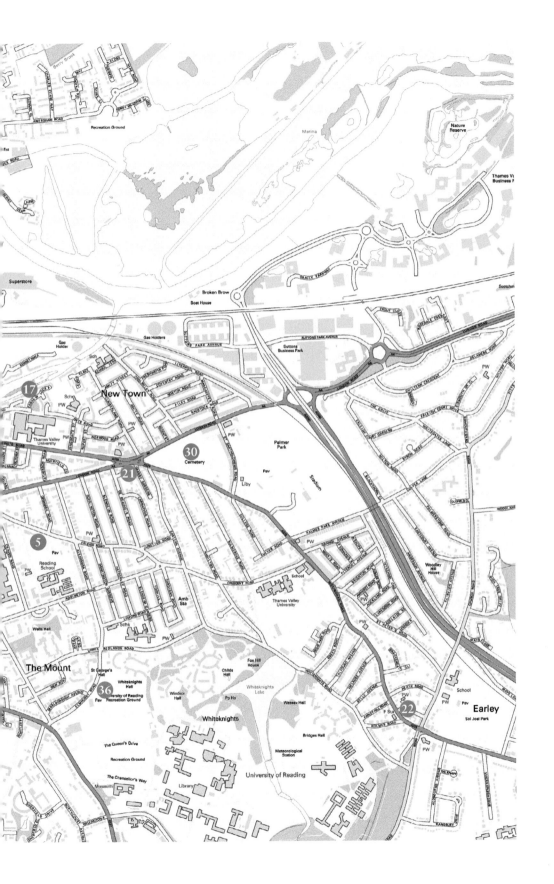

The town hall (1785).

Introduction

'There are many buildings in Reading which we might gladly blow up or burn down, but there are many sacred and hallowed spots.'

A. L. Humphries, *The Streets and Street Lore of Reading* (1926)

The purpose of this book is to tell the story of a town's development through fifty of its most significant buildings. This presents a particular challenge in somewhere like Reading, for the town's economic success over a long period means that built traces of one stage in its history can all too easily be swallowed up in the next round of growth. Looking down the list of buildings featured (*see* overleaf), it is gratifying to see how much of that history has survived. But in a number of cases the town's story lies in the history of the site, rather than necessarily the building that currently occupies it.

As this list also shows, the town's history easily predates the coming of William the Conqueror. But, as far as telling the town's history through its buildings is concerned, the story perhaps begins with Henry I's decision to make Reading the site of an abbey in 1121. This abbey would grow to be one of the richest and most powerful in the land. For four centuries it would dominate the life of the town, all too often at odds with the secular governing bodies trying to run Reading. All of this would come crashing down with the Dissolution of the Monasteries under Henry VIII.

For many years after the Dissolution, Reading's main *raison d'être* was as the focal point of trade for a wide rural catchment area. Then developments in transport – the Kennet and Avon Canal, the turnpike roads and the Great Western Railway – opened up new possibilities for businesses that might otherwise have remained local. The first half of the nineteenth century saw the growth of the town's staple industries – the three Bs – of beer (Simonds), biscuits (Huntley & Palmers) and bulbs (Suttons Seeds). They all grew to be national or international businesses with the help of improved transport and communications. But all three have now left the town, leaving behind scant trace of their presence in the town's buildings.

The town has known its share of conflict over the years, from Alfred the Great fighting the invading Danes, through the Civil War siege of the town's Royalist garrison, to the battle that was fought in Reading's streets during the deposition of James II in 1688. During the Second World War it suffered at least one serious bombing raid, in which almost a hundred people were killed or injured.

Transport has also played its part in the latest stage in the town's history. Since the Second World War, Reading has become one of the region's leading service employment centres – an office boom town. This time the transport innovations were the motor car (with the M4 motorway linking us to London) the aeroplane (with our proximity to Heathrow and Gatwick airports), not to mention the renaissance of the railways, with direct rail access to all corners of the country.

Christ Church (1862).

The 50 Buildings

Minster Church of St Mary the Virgin.

1. Minster Church of St Mary the Virgin (AD 979)

Legend has it that this church dates back to the 630s, when St Birinus founded a small chapel on the site. Ninth-century silver coins have been found in the churchyard, dating from the time when kings Ethelred and Alfred of Wessex fought invading Danes for possession of the town. But the first founding date we can fix with any certainty is 979. In that year Queen Aelfthryth, second wife of Edgar, King of England, founded a nunnery on the site. She did so as a penance for having her stepson Edward murdered at Corfe Castle, to secure the throne for her own son, Ethelred. The nunnery was destroyed in the eleventh century and only a small rounded door from it is said to survive in today's church.

The main body of the church dates from the late eleventh century, and the Domesday Book shows that it, and the surrounding area, were gifted by William the Conqueror to Battle Abbey. In 1121 Henry I founded Reading Abbey and for the next 400 years the abbot was also the rector of St Mary's. This ended with the dissolution of the abbey in 1539 and the Reformation saw the church stripped of much of its ornament. The fabric was however extensively restored between 1551 and 1555, using building materials from the ruined abbey. The pillars separating the south aisle from the nave are said to have come from the abbey.

The church tower featured in the only battle of the misnamed 'bloodless revolution' of 1688, in which William of Orange usurped James II. Irish troops loyal to James used the tower as a lookout to watch for the approach of William's Dutch troops. But townspeople warned the Dutch and brought them into the town via the Oxford Road, giving them the element of surprise. Battle raged in the streets of Reading until the remains of James' force were put to flight.

The church has had further restorations – in 1863 (new choir aisle), 1872, 1918 (war memorial chapel), 1935 and 1997–2003. Most of the church's bells date from the seventeenth and eighteenth centuries and its organ is by the famous Victorian builder, Father Willis. It is a Grade I-listed building.

2. Caversham Park (1047)

The entire history of England could almost be told through the story of Caversham Park. We only have space to touch on a few of the more notable occupants. Before the Norman Conquest it was held by Swein Godwinson, older brother of Harold II. The date 1047 is speculative, being the date of Swein's first exile from England (he died in 1052). William the Conqueror gave the estate to Walter Giffard, a relative who had fought alongside him at Hastings. For a brief while in 1219 all of England was ruled from Caversham Park. The estate was owned at that time by William Marshal, Earl of Pembroke. He had been appointed regent to run the country during the minority of Henry III, and chose to spend his last days doing so from his home.

The royal association continued with owners including the Earl of Warwick, known as the Kingmaker for his part in the deposition of two kings during the Wars of the Roses; Sir Francis Knollys, the Treasurer to Elizabeth I – he and his wife were two of Her Majesty's closest confidants and she was entertained at Caversham Park. The Royalist Earl of Craven also lived there. He had his estates confiscated, and then restored, during the turbulent years of the Civil War and the Restoration. At one time the house served as a prison for Charles I. Other visitors included future US President Thomas Jefferson, who came to see the grounds which, by the time of his visit in 1786, had been landscaped by Lancelot 'Capability' Brown.

Later owners included the Crawshay family, the great ironmasters of Merthyr Tydfil, the Roman Catholic Oratory School and, from 1941, the BBC Monitoring Service. The present house is the fifth or sixth on the estate, and was built after a great fire destroyed

Entrance to the estate today.

Caversham Park, 652.

Caversham Park.

its predecessor in 1850. The current building was by architect Horace (later Sir Horace) Jones, whose other works included Cardiff Town Hall, the London markets of Smithfield, Billingsgate and Leadenshall and, most famously, Tower Bridge. Unsurprisingly, having been commissioned by an ironmaster, the house is built around a fireproof iron frame, though this did not stop it catching fire again, in 1926. The estate was excluded from Reading's 1911 boundary extension, on the grounds that it would never be built upon. But much of it became the Caversham Park Village housing development in the 1960s and today the whole estate is part of Reading.

3. Reading Abbey (1121)

The founding of abbeys was common practice among medieval monarchs, but Reading's was born of personal grief. In November 1120, Prince William, son and heir of Henry I, was drowned off the coast of France and Henry endowed what would be one of the nation's largest and richest abbeys in his memory. Henry laid the foundation stone in 1121 and the abbey church, larger than Westminster Abbey or Winchester Cathedral, was consecrated by Thomas Becket in 1164. Henry had by then died and was buried somewhere within his church.

For the next 400 years the abbey was a great force in the land. It and its relics, including the mummified hand of St James, attracted huge numbers of pilgrims – no shrine in England was its equal. Parliament met there in 1263 and 1453; successive abbots were close confidants of the monarchs, many of whom came to visit; John of Gaunt, third son

Above: The ruins of Reading Abbey today.

Below: Reading Abbey in its former glory.

of Edward III, married there in 1359; and Edward IV announced his secret marriage to Elizabeth Woodville there. By the 1530s it was the sixth wealthiest monastic establishment in England. This said, the relationship between abbey and town was often fraught, and royal intervention was needed to resolve their disputes.

All this came crashing down with Henry VIII's Dissolution of the Monasteries. No serious fault was found with Reading Abbey, but this could not save them. The last abbot, Hugh Cook Farringdon, refused to accept the authority of the king over the church and suffered a brutal public execution in November 1539. The king, his servants and local people stripped the monasteries of their lands, valuables and any useful building materials they would yield. All the dressed stone from Reading Abbey went to other building projects, local or national. What you see today are just the rubbled inner walls.

Centuries of neglect and vandalism were to follow, culminating in an 1831 plan to use the remaining stone walls for road building. This provoked the local newspaper to launch a public subscription to buy, and preserve, the ruins. The council acquired the eastern part of the Forbury in 1854 and the complete gardens as we know them opened in 1873. At the time of writing, the abbey ruins themselves are closed to the public and in need of restoration.

4. St Laurence's Church (*c.* 1121)

The earliest documented reference to St Laurence's is in a charter of Hubert Walter, Bishop of Salisbury between 1189 and 1193. But its origins are probably earlier, making it roughly contemporary with Reading Abbey (hence the speculative date given for its foundation). There is even a suggestion that it preceded the abbey since, until 1557, St Laurence's parishioners were buried in a Saxon graveyard that was within the abbey precincts but actually predated it. The south nave wall and the lower part of the south tower wall of the present church are thought to be early twelfth century.

The building of the new Abbey Hospitium in 1196 is thought to have prompted the enlargement of the church, demolishing the old tower and extending the nave. The current tower dates from 1458 and the north arcade was rebuilt in 1522.

The sixteenth century mathematician John Blagrave paid for a piazza to be built onto the south side of the church. It was used for many years to house the pillory, ducking stool and other instruments of local 'justice', and by day providing comfortable seating for the elderly. But by night it was also a focal point for depravity in the town, until it was demolished in around 1868 as part of a wider refurbishment. Part of the original decorative stonework of the west window, removed in that refurbishment, is displayed in the churchyard. An earlier attachment to that same wall was one of the gateways to the Abbey, above which were small rooms – it was called the Compter and was used as lock-ups for wrongdoers until the nineteenth century.

The church has seen its share of conflict. During the Civil War siege it was pressed into use as a barracks, and had to be refurbished and 'sweetened' afterwards. In 1688 it was the backdrop to the final part of the battle that ended in James II being deposed (*see* 1. Minster Church of St Mary the Virgin). It was also extensively altered in February 1943 when the Luftwaffe dropped a bomb outside, blowing out parts of its west frontage (now restored).

St Laurence's Church.

Part of the original decorative stonework of the former west window.

For a long time, the church was the home of one of three parishes serving medieval Reading, but today it is merged with St Mary's and serves as a mission church, encouraging the faith among the young.

5. Abbey Gateway (c. 1125)

The conjectural date for the Abbey Gateway is that of the signing of the foundation charter for the abbey. The surviving Abbey Gateway is only one of the original entrances to the Abbey Quarter. It marked the boundary between the public areas and those open to monks only. The last abbot, Hugh Faringdon, was executed just outside the gateway.

During the late eighteenth century, the Abbey School used the room above Abbey Gateway as one of their classrooms and early in 1785 two new pupils – nine-year-old Jane Austen and her sister Cassandra – enrolled there. Their stay was a relatively short one; by December 1786 both girls left, since their parents apparently could not afford the expense of keeping them there.

By the early nineteenth century the Abbey Gateway was in a perilous state. It had suffered centuries of neglect, with those repairs that had been undertaken being at best utilitarian and insensitive, and at worst, botched. It was in danger of failure and its appearance was markedly different to what we see today. Belatedly, the council called upon the country's leading Victorian restorer of historic buildings, George Gilbert Scott, to survey it. He had been the architect for the nearby Reading Prison.

Abbey Gateway.

Scott priced the renovation of the gateway at £1,000, which the council grudgingly assembled, but the tender for the work came in at £1,800. This led to renewed calls for its demolition. These were warded off but no more public money was forthcoming. Instead a public appeal was launched for the balance in February 1861. Within hours of this decision, nature intervened with a storm that resulted in the collapse of the gateway. The renovation became a rebuilding programme, the money was raised and the work was finished by 1862. Even so, cost-cutting meant that much of the ornamental stonework on it could not be carved until years later. In 2010 the area had to be closed off when some of the gateway's decorative stonework fell into the street.

Moreover, comparing the early photographic evidence with what we see today suggests that the appearance of the current building may be as much Victorian Gilbert Scott as it is the work of medieval craftsmen.

6. Reading School, Erleigh Road (c. 1125)

Mystery surrounds aspects of the early history of Reading School, such as the date of its foundation. Many possibilities have been put forward, but none is solidly documented. The most likely candidate seems to be 1125, the year Reading Abbey's foundation charter was signed and sealed. If correct, that makes it England's tenth oldest school. It has had a long and sometimes turbulent history, but a book about buildings must concentrate on the school's accommodation.

For its first 400 years the school was part of the abbey, and one of the first references to its precise location is in about 1486. By that time the abbey's hospitium (where they used to entertain visiting pilgrims) was disused, and the abbot (prompted by the king) had proposed converting the building, and the funding that previously went to the hospitium, into a reconstituted 'free school'. Parts of the hospitium refectory remained in school use until the eighteenth century, despite the school's links with the abbey being comprehensively ended by the Dissolution of the Monasteries in 1539.

Reading School, potentially the tenth oldest school in England.

By 1578 the Reading Corporation was looking for new council premises, and the school was the only suitable candidate. The Corporation decided to share the building and an additional floor was built into it. Noise and lack of light became constant bugbears for the school. Matters were not markedly improved when the Corporation built a new town hall building next door, in 1786. The best efforts of the school's most celebrated master, Dr Valpy, to get the school rehoused came to naught until, in 1790, he commissioned a new building on part of the town hall site at his own expense. The school's golden years under Dr Valpy were followed by an equally rapid decline under his son as headmaster. By 1865 the school had just six pupils.

The Reading School Act of 1867 gave parliamentary approval for a modern grammar school on a new site. But the authorities only had less than £5,000 of the estimated £25,000 cost of the project. Undeterred, they negotiated the purchase of 10 acres of land at Erleigh Road and hired the distinguished architect Alfred Waterhouse to design the new buildings. It only got built after the council underwrote a massive mortgage for much of the cost. Repaying it would plunge the school into years of financial crisis, from which they finally defaulted in 1908.

7. St Peter's Church, Caversham (c. 1162)

The early history of Caversham's main church is intermingled with that of a shrine. The Shrine of Our Lady of Caversham was thought to have been located somewhere near the

St Peter's Church.

The surviving
twelfth-century door.

church. An early reference to them both appears in a document dated 1199 from King John, referring to 'the church of Kaversham together with the Chapel of the blessed Virgin Mary and all things pertaining to them'. But church and shrine are both thought to have existed long before then. Our speculative date for it is based on an early documented reference. One possibility is that the site for the church, which is not exactly central to the Caversham of old, was chosen specifically to adjoin the shrine.

The widow of the first Earl of Buckingham (from 1066 the Lord of the Manor of Caversham) is thought to have donated an important holy relic to the shrine in 1106. Its collection of relics included what was said to be the rope with which Judas hanged himself and part of the spear that pierced Jesus' side during the crucifixion. It drew large numbers of pilgrims to the shrine, including Henry VIII's wife, Catherine of Aragon, in 1532. Some pilgrims claimed to experience miraculous cures. As for the church and its land-holding, the third Earl is said to have donated them to Notley Abbey in Buckinghamshire in 1162. The shrine was supposed to have been housed in St Peter's Church at some stage in its life, but all trace of it was lost by the time of the dissolution of Notley Abbey in 1538.

During the Civil War siege, Royalist troops installed a cannon on the top of the church tower. Both the tower and much of the rest of the church were wrecked in the exchange of fire that followed. The tower was replaced by a wooden structure, which was seriously dilapidated by 1878/9 when the present flint building took its place. The main body of the church was enlarged at the same time, as a response to Caversham's growing population. A further chapel was added in 1924 as a First World War memorial. The south doorway from the twelfth-century church survives.

8. Reading Abbey Hospitium (1189)

Reading's great abbey church and its collection of holy relics (promising miraculous cures) made it one of medieval England's leading places of pilgrimage. Caring for the needs of their pilgrims was one of the most important responsibilities of the abbey and they soon found that that the facilities they had built for it in the 1120s were completely overwhelmed by the volume of visitors. The hospitium (where they entertained guests) was rebuilt on a grand scale between 1189 and 1193, with a refectory of 120 feet by 20–30 feet wide, which stood roughly on the site today occupied by the old Town Hall. At right angles to it, and roughly along the line of modern-day Valpy Street, was a 200-foot dormitory, capable of sleeping around 400 pilgrims.

The practice of pilgrimage declined in the later medieval period and the hospitium was suppressed by 1480. Following an intervention by the king, the refectory was pressed into use in around 1486 as a schoolroom for what would eventually become Reading School. By 1578 the Corporation were looking for a new town hall, and they decided to provide it by inserting an additional floor above the schoolroom, an arrangement that was not ideal for either party. The remains of the hospitium fronting modern Blagrave Street were demolished in 1786, and the site eventually redeveloped.

Meanwhile, following the Dissolution of the Monasteries, the hospitium's dormitory was used as a stable and, during the Civil war, as a barracks for the besieged Royalist troops. After a long period of decline, the dilapidated remains of the dormitory were

The remains of the hospitium, seen from St Laurence's churchyard.

bought by the Corporation. Pressure to demolish them was resisted and they were renovated and adapted in 1892 by architect Slingsby Stallwood. For a time they were the home for laboratories for the Reading Extension College, forerunner to the University of Reading.

They were further refurbished as part of a modern office development and since 2011 have been home to a day nursery. What remains of the hospitium today can be seen from St Laurence's churchyard.

The former Reading Abbey hospitium, currently in use a day nursery.

9. St Michael's Church, Routh Lane, Tilehurst (1189)

There has been a church in Tilehurst since the twelfth century, though the earliest one would have been a wooden structure, of which no trace now survives. The earliest documented reference to it was in a charter by the Bishop of Salisbury, issued somewhere between 1189 and 1193. The earliest surviving part of the church is the South Aisle, now the Lady Chapel, built in the late 13th or early 14th century. This aisle contains brasses commemorating Gauwin More and his wife Isabella, both of whom died around 1469. Gauwin was the son of Richard, a marshal in Henry VI's court. Other extensions were added to the church over the years, including the square tower, dating from 1730.

In 1855 the church underwent, more or less, a complete rebuild, paid for by the Routh family, two of whom were Rectors of Tilehurst between 1810 to 1905. The South Aisle and the tower were retained (it was at this point that the tower got its

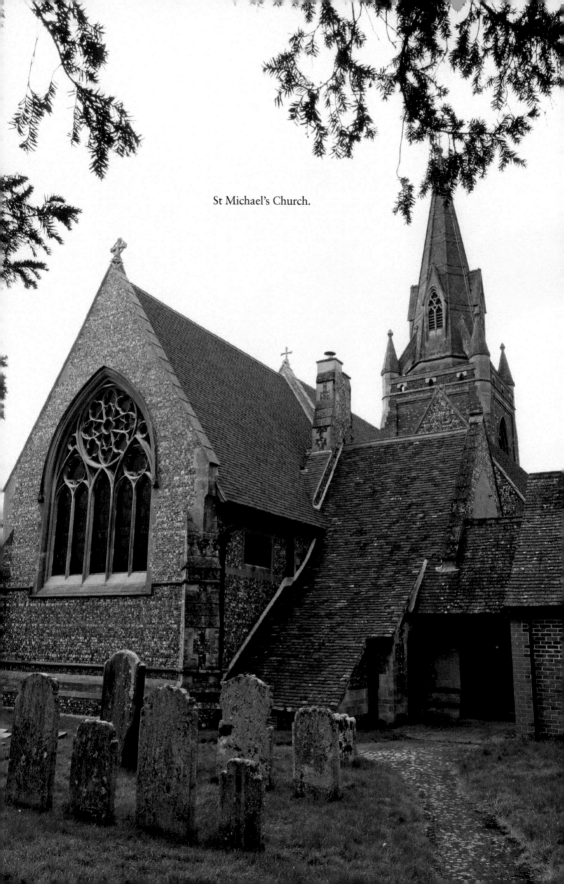

St Michael's Church.

The square tower – an addition to the church dating to 1730.

spire) but the rest was rebuilt to a design by the eminent architect George Edmund Street (1824–81). He was one of the leading lights in the Victorian Gothic revival, best known for the Royal Courts of Justice in the Strand, although the bulk of his work consisted of churches. For a time, he was diocesan architect for Oxford and in later life was Professor of Architecture to the Royal Academy. He was buried in Westminster Abbey. Another eminent designer represented in the church is William Morris, who was responsible for the east window. Street was a friend of the Pre-Raphaelites and Morris was once his pupil.

Also commemorated in the south aisle is Sir Peter Vanlore. He was born in Holland in 1547, became a banker and moneylender and came to England as a Protestant refugee. He became Lord of the Manor of Tilehurst in 1604, a naturalised Englishman in 1607 and was knighted by James I in 1621. He married the daughter of a wealthy London merchant, Jacoba Thibault and they set up home in a house on the site of the present Calcot House. He died in 1627, the father of a son and ten daughters, and in 1638 a son-in-law erected the monument to his memory.

10. St Giles' Church, Southampton Street (1191)

St Giles' Church has its origins in the twelfth century. The first written reference to it was in a document of 1191, in which Pope Clement III gave the church (along with nearby St Mary's) to the Abbot of Reading. It was originally built within St Mary's parish as a 'chapel of ease'. That is, it was built to serve to serve the population south of the River Kennet, who would have found it difficult to attend services at St Mary's for much of the year (this part of the Kennet was at that time divided into seven streams, separated by muddy islands).

The church (and its ministers) have been involved in some of the more dramatic parts of the town's history. In 1539 the church's priest, John Enyon, sided with the abbot of Reading, Hugh Cook Faringdon, in opposing Henry VIII's claim to be the head of the church in England. He was found guilty on a trumped-up charge of treason and hanged in front of the abbey gateway. Far less inspirational was the impact of another minister, Joseph Ayre. He succeeded two popular and evangelical vicars and his brand of 'tepid rationalism' had the congregation leaving in droves. This led to the founding of the new St Mary's Church in Castle Street.

During the Civil War, Reading was in Royalist hands. They fortified the town, which was besieged by parliamentary forces. As part of the fortifications the Royalists installed guns in St Giles' church tower. This naturally attracted the attention of the parliamentary artillery and the upper part of the church tower, including the spire, was destroyed in 1643. It was restored at the end of the war, with the results seen in an early (1840s) picture by the photographic pioneer William Henry Fox-Talbot.

The church underwent a more fundamental 'restoration' in 1872–73 at the hands of architect James Piers St Aubyn (1815–95). As one modern critic put it, 'the rather pleasant old-fashioned church was remodelled into a very ordinary Victorian building.' Only the thirteenth-century aisle walls and perpendicular-style west tower survived. The transepts, chancel, chancel aisles and the present spire were all Victorian additions, and even some of the surviving original walls were encased in flint.

St Giles' Church.

St Giles' churchyard.

11. Greyfriars Church, Friar Street (1311)

In 1233 a group of Franciscan monks in grey robes arrived in Reading to minister to the poor. They had no money but carried authority from the pope, instructing the abbot of Reading to find them a site for their church. The abbot had little choice but to assist this rival organisation, however unwillingly. He found them a site prone to flooding by Caversham Bridge, itself cut off from the town by a road (Watery Lane, today's Caversham Road) that was frequently flooded (it took over 1,000 wagons of gravel to lift the road out of the floodplain in the 1720s). Unsurprisingly, the site proved unviable and, with the help of a more supportive archbishop of Canterbury, the friars secured their present site, at Town's End, the end of Friar Street, in 1288. There they built Greyfriars Church, completed in 1311.

Over two centuries of worship at Greyfriars came to an end in 1538 with the Dissolution of the Monasteries. Government-sponsored looting and private enterprise quickly stripped the building of much of its useful building materials, and what was left was pressed into service in 1543 as the town's guildhall. This use continued until about 1578, after which it became in turn a hospital and workhouse, and then a particularly inhuman prison, in which the inmates were treated worse than animals. Even this use ceased with the opening of the new county gaol in 1844, and the town was left with a roofless disused shell.

A local Catholic named James Wheble had tried to buy it in the 1830s, as a basis for their place of worship following Catholic emancipation in 1829, but he was rejected as a

Greyfriars Church.

The church prior to restoration.

purchaser (see the entry on St James' Church). It was not until 1863 that the building finally restored as a church. This was undertaken by W. H. Woodman, at that time the borough surveyor, at a cost of £12,000. Although parts of the church had been totally destroyed and could not be included in the restoration, it stands today as the most complete surviving example of Franciscan architecture in England, the oldest Franciscan church still used as a place of worship and a Grade I-listed building.

12. George Inn, King Street (c. 1423)

Old Reading had no shortage of places of refreshment. A census from 1577, conducted for taxation purposes, established that there were fifty-four drinking establishments for a population of around 3,000 – one alehouse for every fifty-five men, women and children in the town. One of the oldest survivors of these is the George in King Street. Quite how old is another matter, for sources variously date it back to 1506, 1423 or earlier. The date 1423 relates to Richard Bedewynde's will, the town's mayor between 1385 and 1388, who left 'the reversion of the tenement called the Georgesyn in Reading to the Mayor of the vill of Reding for the time being', so it must have existed prior to the will. In 1512/13 a payment of 5d (2p) was made to the George for 'bere and ale to my Lord Chamberleyns' and in the late

The hotel entrance.

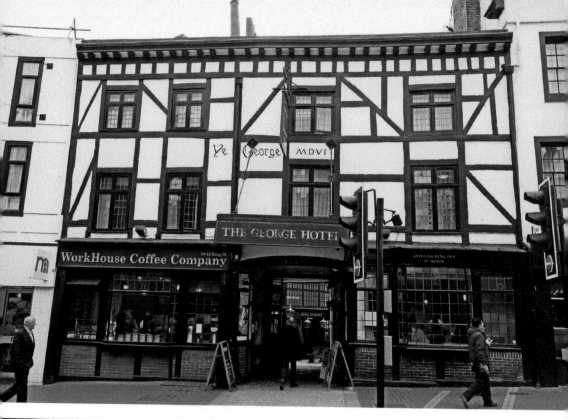

Above: The George Inn, which dates to the early fifteenth century.

Left: The alley that leads to the entrance to the hotel.

1540s the establishment passed to William Gray, a friend of the Lord Protector Somerset, who was responsible for the systematic pillaging of Reading Abbey after its dissolution in 1539. The inn was said to have been the scene of a skirmish between Roundheads and Cavaliers during the Civil War.

Famous visitors to Reading have stayed at several of its old inns. Samuel Pepys lodged at the Broad Face in High Street; the poet Coleridge was billeted at the Bear in Bridge Street under the improbable pseudonym Silas Tomkins Comberpatch while serving in the 15th Light Dragoons and on the run from his creditors; and religious reformer John Wesley made the Crown in Crown Street his watering hole of choice. The George allegedly hosted Charles Dickens, who used it as a staging post while travelling to his speaking engagements around the country. It would also have been conveniently close to the Mechanics' Institution in London Street, where Dickens performed on more than one occasion.

The George long predated the golden age of coaching, but became a coaching inn. Hones General Coach Office was next door, offering daily coach services to over thirty destinations. Among the services departing from there were the Telegraph (to London via Maidenhead), the Rocket (to Southampton) and the Star (to Bath and Bristol).

Most of what survives of the George today is eighteenth or nineteenth century, apart from a ghost alleged by some to haunt the premises, who is a Cavalier of Civil War vintage.

13. Vachel Almshouses, Castle Street (1634)

The Vachels (or Vachells) were one of Reading's leading families, associated with the town since at least 1261. Sir Thomas Vachell was one of Reading's Members of Parliament

The Vachel almshouses.

One of the almshouses prior to their development.

from 1529 onwards, and was an active supporter of Thomas Cromwell in the dissolution of Reading Abbey. In 1634 another Thomas Vachel commissioned some almshouses in St Mary's Butts, (named St Mary's Almshouses) for 'six aged and impotent men, without wives'. He endowed the properties with £40 a year to maintain the occupants. Each one got 2s a week and two loads of wood per year.

By 1867 the houses were nearing the end of their useful lives. The site was sold and the proceeds, along with public subscriptions and money from municipal charities, were used to fund the development of the almshouses on Castle Street. They were named after the original benefactor, were designed by William Henry Woodman and were themselves modernised in 1960–02. They are today Grade II-listed buildings and the plaque from the original almshouses is displayed on them.

14. Broad Street Independent Chapel (1662/1707)

There was long-standing opposition to the established church in Reading. As early as 1416 the Lollards campaigned locally for a simpler, more direct form of religion, freed from embelleshments, Latin and the mediation of priests. The Establishment strongly opposed this heresy and there were few figures more establishment than William Laud. Born in

The former Broad Street Independent Chapel, now a Waterstones store.

The interior of Waterstones, showing hints of the building's former use as a chapel.

1573 near the junction of Broad Street and what is now Queen Victoria Street, he rose to become very high in the Church and intolerant Archbishop of Canterbury. He was executed for treason by Cromwell's Parliament in 1645. The Act of Uniformity (1662) imposed fines, imprisonment or transportation on those who worshipped outside the Church of England.

Nonconformists had to worship in secret. In Reading a Mrs Thorn, wife of a tanner in Mill Lane, kept two ministers concealed in her premises, from which they crept to conduct their services when nobody in authority was watching. Religious orthodoxy was not to be relaxed until William and Mary assumed the throne and passed the Toleration Act of 1689. This at least allowed some limited freedom of worship, under licence.

The original Broad Street Chapel dates from 1707, but bears the date 1662 on its front entrance. This date is conjectural, and appears to represent a symbolic start for independent worship in Reading. It was when one Christopher Fowler – having been expelled from St Mary's for his refusal to conform – started conducting private ceremonies in his own home. In that year, the mayor of Reading complained that 'by [Fowler's] meetings the audiences in the Churches are made very thin. The schismatics scorn persuasion and defy powers'.

The original building was set back from Broad Street. It was roughly square with a domed ceiling with first-floor galleries round its walls. In 1892 a separate building was erected, fronting onto Broad Street, incorporating an arch and tower, and shops on either side of the archway.

The church survived as a place of worship until 1984, when a final service was held and the building was left, vacant and deteriorating, for much of the next decade. Various schemes to refurbish the listed building came and went until the book chain store, Waterstones, took it on. It proved an ideal use but the conversion was not straightforward, with 148 buried bodies found beneath the church having to be reinterred elsewhere. The building finally reopened as a bookshop in November 1995.

15. Watlington House, Watlington Street (1688)

The earliest surviving map of Reading, dating from 1611, shows an unmade tree-lined avenue running from the River Kennet to London Road, near what is now Redlands Road. This would one day be Watlington Street. The Watlingtons were leading figures in the civic life of Reading for two centuries. The earliest reference to them was in 1520, and various Watlingtons were mayors of Reading on at least nine occasions between 1574 and 1710. Samuel Watlington (mayor in 1695 and 1710) built Watlington House in 1688. It was originally only half its present size, the front half being added in about 1763. Some claim it to be the oldest surviving residential property in the borough.

The family occupied the house for around 100 years, but it is not exactly clear when they left. In 1794 the Corporation (the ground landlords) let it to a soldier, Captain Edward Purvis, who was later to fight in the Battle of Corunna where he was shot (but only through the hat!). Purvis is now said to haunt the house, and is allegedly seen sitting at the window in military attire, smoking his pipe. Other occupants over the years have included 'an establishment for young ladies', Kendrick Girls' School (between 1877 and 1927) and a range of charities.

Front view of the seventeenth-century building Watlington House. *Inset*: Some of the original beams inside.

Rear view of the house and its garden.

16. The Sun Inn, Castle Street

The Sun, originally thought to have been called the Rising Sun, was developed into an inn in around 1700. The inn was noted for its underground accommodation, possibly in part the remains of cells from the medieval prison next door, or a survival from an adjoining ancient friary. John Leland, who visited the town in the 1540s, spoke of a 'late fayre house of the Grey Friars in Castle Strete'.

Whatever its origins, this underground accommodation, which was used for stabling up to fifty horses, was right below the bedrooms, which cannot have done much for the amenities of their guests. In more modern times, when stabling for horses was no longer required, other things were stored there. In 1947 it provided shelter for Bertram Mills' circus, including their elephants. The elephants' rampaging brought about the structural collapse of part of the building.

The Sun was not a coaching inn, but it was frequented by carriers, right up until the 1940s. Wilder speculations, like it being the site of Reading's long-lost castle, or there being secret tunnels from there to the abbey, seem safer to dismiss, though there was a passage called Grape Lane, that ran from Castle Street to Hosier Street as long ago as 1347.

The Sun Inn.

17. Blake's Lock and the Kennet and Avon Canal (1720)

Blake's Lock, the first lock on the Kennet and Avon Canal, reminds us of the part the river that became the canal played in the life of the town. It also recalls a major piece of civil disorder on the part of the townspeople. From its earliest days the town was dependent upon its waterways as a channel of trade and communication – the medieval abbey derived a substantial income from its control of waterborne trade. Reading was fortunate in being the limit of navigation for most boats along the Kennet, and benefited from much of the area's trade being channelled through the town.

There had been talk since Elizabethan times of using the rivers Kennet and Avon as parts of a canal between Bristol and London. A first step to achieve this was taken in 1715, when the Kennet Navigation Act was passed, permitting the river between Reading and Newbury to be made navigable. Reading people feared this would lose them their pre-eminent trading position and in 1720 their opposition turned to violence. A mob of around 300 citizens, led by their mayor, Robert Blake (not the same Blake after whom the lock is named), tried to destroy part of the canal works. They failed, and the canal opened between Reading and Newbury in 1723. The citizens then took to stoning bargees passing through the town and issuing them with death threats. But it soon became clear that, far from the canal harming the local economy, Reading was enjoying a new period of prosperity because of it.

The Kennet and Avon Canal to Bristol was approved in 1794 and completed in 1810. Other linked canals also opened, giving Reading access to large parts of the nation, to sell its goods and buy in other people's more cheaply. But the Kennet and Avon's golden years were short. The Great Western Railway reached Bristol in 1841 and the canal was doomed. A long period of decline and abandonment was to follow, which was only reversed when the canal was restored and reopened for leisure use in 1990.

Blake's Lock.

18. Prospect Park Mansion House (1757)

What we now know as Prospect Park, the setting for Mansion House, was once part of the much larger Calcot Park estate. The house at Calcot Park was the original manor house of Tilehurst Manor. It was later the home of 'the Berkshire Lady', Frances Kendrick. She was rich, beautiful, sweet-natured and – most unusual of all – a free agent in matters matrimonial. She turned down many suitors who failed to meet her standards, and developed an undeserved reputation as a heart-breaker. She finally fell in love with an impoverished barrister, Benjamin Childs, who had not wooed her on the grounds that he thought himself unworthy of such a prize. She won his hand by the unusual means of challenging him (in disguise) to wed him or fight him in a duel. He chose matrimony and they were married at St Mary's Wargrave in 1707.

Their happiness together at Calcot Park was short-lived, for Frances died in 1722. The widowed Benjamin later sold much of the estate, but retained the eastern part, on which stood a farmhouse, Dirle's Farm. This he remodelled from 1757 into what would eventually become Mansion House. He named Prospect Park for its views over Reading. The house was bought and greatly extended in about 1800 by John Englebert Liebenrood. He added the east and west wings, the colonnaded portico and other features and had the building finished in stucco.

Prospect Park Mansion House.

Towards the end of the century the estate came into the ownership of J. C. Fidler, a leading local businessman and councillor, to whom Reading owes many debts of gratitude. In 1901 he encouraged and enabled the council to buy the estate, offering it to them at the relatively knock-down price for 63 acres of £13,850 for the benefit of weary workers who, when at rest, needed some open space where communion with nature might be established. He even contributed the first £1,000 of the purchase price.

Over the years Prospect Park survived most pressures for other uses (such as in 1904, for a municipal cemetery, though not in 1906 for an isolation hospital). Mansion House itself was used for park-related activities such as changing rooms and refreshments for park users, while falling into dereliction through lack of maintenance. In the 1980s it was renovated for use as a restaurant.

19. Boar's Head Inn, Friar Street (1760)

1760 is the earliest recorded reference to the fondly remembered Boar's Head in Friar Street, (disrespectfully known to some of its customers as 'the Whore's Bed') and its owner Thomas Flavey, a former mayor of Reading. In 1785 it was acquired by brewer and public house owner William Garrard (who gave his name to Garrard Street). The Garrard family would later sell it to the Courage brewing empire. But in 1840 one day's drinking was interrupted by the arrival of a crowd bearing the dead body of Henry West. He was a young carpenter who had been swept from the roof of the brand-new Reading railway station, on which he had been working, by a freak whirlwind. He was laid out in the bar while an inquest was conducted. A wooden memorial in St Laurence's Church commemorates Henry West.

The pub itself survived until 2004, when it was replaced by a large and anonymous hotel, and its distinctive three-dimensional signage – the Boar's Head - is now looked after by the town's museum service.

The Boar's Head Inn.

The wooden memorial in St Laurence's Church which commemorates Henry West.

2c. Reading Old Town Hall (1785)

Reading's seat of local government has had a fairly mobile existence over the centuries. Its earliest home was next to the River Kennet, where the Oracle shopping development now sits. Unfortunately, it was next to where the town's housewives did their laundry, and the noise from this drowned out the deliberations of the town's dignitaries. Later they occupied what was left of the Greyfriars Church and later still part of the Abbey Hospitium. By 1785 the abbey building was showing signs of structural failure and a new one was commissioned.

The designer was Charles Poulton, an alderman of the council and not an architect but a cabinet maker. His building, which cost £1,800, survives to this day as the Victoria Hall, the first part of the Town Hall complex. For the old town hall is not one building but four, built by different architects over the course of more than a century. Phase two was designed by the local, but nationally famous, architect, Alfred Waterhouse, and was completed by 1875. Among his previous commissions had been the world's most expensive building, Manchester Town Hall.

The council rapidly outgrew phase two and an architectural competition was organised in 1882 for the design of phase three. The contest was overseen by another architect, Thomas Lainson, and Waterhouse was again an entrant. When Waterhouse's design proved too expensive, Lainson caused a controversy by awarding the contract to himself.

Phase four, housing the art gallery and library extension, opened in 1897, was designed by yet another architect, W. R. Howell. The last two phases were largely funded by public subscription, with the biscuit-making Palmer family prominent among the list of contributors.

By the 1970s, most local authority activity had moved out of the complex and there were pressures for its demolition. Public outcry followed, including the formation of Reading Civic Society. It was finally agreed to refurbish it as an arts and conference centre, and the great concert hall opened at the very start of the new millennium.

Above: Reading Old Town Hall.

Left: Detail of the buildings.

21. Marquis of Granby, Cemetery Junction (1786)

This pub was originally known as the Gallows Tavern, being the last port of call for prisoners en route to their appointment with the nearby gallows (more than one Reading hostelry claims this dubious distinction). On a lighter note, it was the setting for Reading's first venture into theatrical entertainment. In October 1786, Mrs White, proprietor of the Maidenhead Theatre, chose the pub as the venue for a new theatre. It did good business for about a month, until thieves stole most of their costumes. They never recovered from the loss. The pub no doubt predates this enterprise.

The Marquis of Granby probably has more pubs named after him than any other non-royal person. John Manners, Marquis of Granby (1721–1770) was the eldest son of the third Duke of Rutland and had a successful career as a soldier, commanding the troops on the battlefield during the Seven Years' War. He was later made Commander-in-Chief of the Armed Forces. Known to be fond of a drink, he was in the habit of setting up his old soldiers as pub licensees once they were too old to fight. Many a grateful landlord named their pub after their old commanding officer. However, his generosity meant that he died with debts of £37,000.

The Marquis of Granby public house.

22. St Mary's Church, Castle Street (1798)

In the early medieval period almost anybody could run a prison and they were virtually unregulated. Reading had a number – the Compter, part of the gateway to Reading Abbey, next to St Laurence's Church; the Hole, a single cell built into the end of the Blagrave Piazza (*see* 4. St Laurence's Church) and a lock-up at the rear of the Shades public house in Gun Street.

In 1403 Henry IV determined that Justices of the Peace should only incarcerate prisoners in the common gaol, run by the county sheriff. Reading's county gaol was in Castle Street and consisted of a series of subterranean cells, from which the prisoners could beg through a grating in the street. This they needed to do, to raise finance, since most of the necessities of life beyond the most basic had to be bought from the gaoler. The inmates – which included debtors, felons, people of unsound mind, religious dissenters and newly press-ganged 'recruits' to the Royal Navy – lived in conditions that were overcrowded, largely unsegregated by sex and thoroughly insanitary.

The site was vacated when a new house of correction was provided on the site of the present Reading Gaol. As we saw, the new occupants of the site were most of the congregation of St Giles Church. They had been driven from their place of worship by an extremely uncharismatic new clergyman, Joseph Ayres. He succeeded a couple of popular and evangelistic incumbents, and his brand of tepid rationalism (one of his sermons was on the theme of 'The probable causes and consequences of Enthusiasm') did not go down at all well. By December 1798 deserters from the congregation were able to fill a 1,000-seat chapel in Castle Street.

St Mary's Church.

The church started out as a simple Georgian building but, in 1840, local architect Henry Briant added the portico, made of coade stone (a form of manufactured building material) in the Corinthian style. The building itself is finished in stucco. The building has a fine galleried interior and is listed Grade II. Today's congregation is part of the Continuing Anglican movement (which was founded at this church in 1994 and practises a conservative form of Anglican worship, based on the 1662 Book of Common Prayer).

23. The Three Tuns, Wokingham Road (1798)

The Three Tuns reminds us of the only Prime Minister Reading ever produced and his links with Reading. Henry Addington was the son of a successful doctor, based in London Street, through whom Henry became childhood friends with William Pitt the Younger. Pitt encouraged Henry into politics, and he became Member of Parliament, Speaker of the House of Commons and, from 1801, Prime Minister. He was forced out of office in 1804, but a long career in politics followed, including ten years as Home Secretary in which he ruthlessly crushed all dissent.

When Napoleon threatened invasion in the 1790s the regular British Army was reinforced by newly formed troops of volunteers (forerunners of the Territorial Army). Those who owned a horse could volunteer for the cavalry, rather than the infantry. Among the first to form in Berkshire, in 1798, were the Woodley Cavalry, commanded from 1798 to 1806 by one Capt. Henry Addington. They would practise drill one day and one evening a week and their headquarters was the Three Tuns. The pub that occupied the site then has since been replaced, but the use of the site (drinking, that is, not soldiering) and the name survive.

The Three Tuns.

Lord Sidmaith

Painted by John Copley, Esq R.A

Engraved by E. Finden

Henry Addington

The Three Tuns.

24. Simonds Bank, King Street (1814)

This building reminds us of one of Reading's more colourful families of entrepreneurs. But first, what of King Street, on which it stands? The street was created in the mid-eighteenth century when the row of cottages down the middle, separating it into Sun Lane and Back Lane was demolished, by a draper named John Richards. He named the new street in honour of George III.

William Blackall Simonds (1761–1834) was born into money and increased his wealth by marrying the daughter of a brewer from Basingstoke. He used it to establish a state of the art brewery on part of the site now occupied by the Oracle shopping centre. The growth of his business was severely curtailed by a cartel of the town's established brewers, which prevented him from competing. Things got so bad that by 1814 he considered quitting brewing and concentrating on banking, setting up his business in King Street. The surviving building, dating from 1838–39, is by local architects Henry and Nathaniel Briant.

He handed the brewing business to his son Blackall, a man of robust business practices. He was by no means above bribing his rivals and threatened to fight a duel with at least one other entrepreneur who crossed him. Blackall's circle of friends (and political allies) included the then Prime Minister, the Duke of Wellington. Through him, Simonds got to hear of the forthcoming Beer Act that would break monopolies like the one in Reading. He used his love of hunting to scour the countryside for potential pub sites, finding fifty by the time the bill became law in 1830. Simonds did not look back from this beginning, and his

Left: Simonds Bank.

Below: Simonds Bank.

King Street, Reading
looking east

brewing business grew to be one of the country's largest, until it was swallowed into the even larger Courage empire in 1960.

An artistic member of the Simonds family, George Blackall Simonds, made his own contribution to the town as a sculptor, being responsible for the town's statues of the Forbury Lion, Queen Victoria and Edward VII. As for the banking business, it became part of Barclays in 1913. The building, vacant at the time of writing, for a long time still had the Simonds brass nameplate on its door.

25. Huntley & Palmers (1822)

Today, a small building fronting onto Kings Road is all that remains of what was once the world's largest biscuit factory, employing several thousand staff. But Huntley & Palmers' presence in the town is marked in so many other ways – the park that bears the Palmer name, the university, the museum and art gallery, all of which they helped to fund.

The business was started in 1822 by Joseph Huntley from a small shop in London Street, selling biscuits to the town's growing middle-class clientele and to stagecoach passengers at the nearby Crown Hotel. Three factors helped the business to grow from local to international. One was the development of transport – the canals and railways. A second was Joseph's second son going into the business of making tinplate boxes, which proved ideal for keeping the biscuits fresh. The third was the entrepreneurial genius of George Palmer, with whom Huntley went into partnership in 1841. At the time the Huntley and Palmer partnership was formed the company was valued at just over £1,000, £750 of which was in unpaid debts owed them.

Huntley & Palmers today.

An early image of Huntley & Palmers.

Palmer developed all sorts of machinery for automating biscuit production and set up a national network of commission agents. By 1846 they were able to establish their own factory, near the railway and the canal. Turnover grew rapidly to £105,000 in around 1855, and by 1860 they were the biggest biscuit manufacturer in the land.

They started exporting biscuits as early as 1844 and by the mid-1850s 15 per cent of production went overseas. They reached the farthest and most exotic parts of the world, kept fresh in their tinplate boxes. By the end of the nineteenth century they were the town's largest employer and the world's largest biscuit maker.

The company's meteoric rise in the nineteenth century was matched by a long decline in the twentieth, as they were hit by two world wars, increased competition, obsolete manufacturing equipment and unadventurous management. The manufacturing of biscuits in Reading ceased in 1977 and the administrative offices left town a few years later.

26. Reading Mechanics' Institution, London Street (1825)

Reading Mechanics' Institution was formed in 1825 'to open to the view of the Artisan the truths of Natural Philosophy and Science'. It constantly ran at a loss and closed in 1830. It was reborn in 1840, this time with Prince Albert as a patron, and permanent premises were acquired in London Street. By 1843 it had broadened its remit to cover science and literature, and was known as the Reading Literary Scientific and Mechanics' Institution. In 1853 it was converted into the Theatre Royal. Charles Dickens was among those who

Reading Mechanics' Institution.

appeared there, to read extracts from his works but, by the 1860s, audiences were falling and it was sold on to the Primitive Methodists in 1866.

They too eventually abandoned the building and in 1950 the Everyman Theatre Company persuaded the council to buy it and lease it to them as a theatre. They survived until 1957 and in 1960 the Reading Newspaper Company became the next owner of the building. Today it is used as a hotel and bar, retaining its Ionic columned front and the name 'Great Expectations' to reflect its Dickensian associations.

27. Royal Berkshire Hospital (1839)

It took almost a century for the idea of a hospital to take root in Reading, as economisers and those with vested interests in health care combined to talk down the idea. But before it did, there was at least the Reading Dispensary. From 1802 this opened one hour a day, three days a week, to dispense medicines and treatment to those deemed 'worthy objects of charity'. Within a year, they were able to obtain premises in Chain Street and appoint a resident dispenser. As the population and the demand for treatment grew, the idea of a hospital gained momentum.

This idea owed much to the efforts of Edward Oliver, a retired bank clerk, who walked the length of Berkshire from 1830 onwards, drumming up support from everyone from the king (whose patronage gave it the title 'Royal') downwards. One convert was Reading's only Prime Minister, Henry Addington, now Lord Sidmouth. After initially opposing the idea,

Royal Berkshire Hospital.

he was sufficiently persuaded that he did not just sell, but gave, the hospital the site on which it now stands. An architectural competition was held, which was won by local architect Henry Briant. He submitted two entries, both of which reached the final three, and was invited to build the elevations of one on the floorplan of the other. The actual building costs exceeded the limit set in the competition brief (£6,000) by over 50 per cent.

The grand opening took place in May 1839. Such was the demand for its services, partly due to the accident-prone construction of the Great Western Railway nearby, that the hospital nearly doubled in size in its first eleven years. Its subsequent history was a long struggle to fund and accommodate the growing demands of an increasing population and the ever-increasing sophistication of medical science. Until the days of the NHS this depended upon voluntary donations.

Other facilities were pressed into service; from 1906 a fever hospital was opened next to Prospect Park and, from the First World War onwards, Reading Workhouse began its transformation into Battle Hospital. In both world wars they faced the added burden of treating large numbers of war wounded including, in the Second World War, civilian casualties. 1948 saw the hospital become part of the new National Health Service, but it took until 2005 for all the town's hospital facilities to be concentrated onto the Royal Berks site.

28. St James' Church, Forbury Road (1840)

Catholicism was for a long time outlawed in Britain. The Catholic Relief Act of 1791 eased their persecution somewhat, but there were still strict controls on their worship. Before the Act a Mrs Stuart rented a room in Minster Street, where mass was said illegally, and a room in Finch's Buildings, Hosier Lane was converted into a legal place of worship in 1791. But by Victorian times Catholics in Reading still had no proper place of worship of their own.

Most of the landowners around Reading were Catholic, but a leading light of the local Catholic community was James Wheble of Bulmershe Court, Sheriff of Berkshire and Lord of the Manor of Bulmershe. As we saw, he tried to buy the ruins of Greyfriars Church for restoration as a Catholic church, but was rebuffed by the owners. He turned instead to part of the site of the ruined abbey, fronting onto Forbury Road.

Having acquired the site, he engaged the eminent architect (and Catholic) Augustus Welby Pugin for what would be one of the first, if not the first, of his church commissions. His other work included St Chad's Cathedral, Birmingham and a share in the design of the Houses of Parliament. The design of this church is unusual for its Romanesque architecture, given that Pugin was strongly of the view that neo-Gothic was the correct style for churches. It is thought that he may have wanted it to blend in with the neighbouring abbey ruins. The laying of the foundation stone, on 14 December 1837, was the first public Catholic service in Reading since the Reformation, and was attended by between 2,000–3,000 people.

There was local opposition to the church, on the surface due to a dispute about a right of way across the site. But how far this was underpinned by anti-Catholic opinion is impossible to say. The church opened on 5 August 1840, but the ceremony was marred by the death from a heart attack of James Wheble, three weeks before the event. In a final gesture in his will, Wheble donated the church and its land to the church authorities. The church was added to in 1925 and 1962, and is today a Grade II-listed building.

Detail on St James' Church.

St James' Church.

29. Reading Railway Station (1840)

The Victorian remains of the railway station remind us of the contribution the railways made to the industrial growth of the town in the nineteenth century. To varying degrees all three of the town's staple Victorian industries – beer, biscuits and bulbs – relied upon the railways to distribute their wares to their national and international markets.

After a long legal battle, Great Western Railway got parliamentary approval to build their railway between London and Bristol – via Reading – in 1835. It reached Reading in 1840. The railway's engineer, Isambard Kingdom Brunel, had a revolutionary idea for Reading's station. Because almost all of the town's population then lived to the south of the railway, Brunel built it with both platforms on the same side of the tracks. It was convenient for the passengers but dangerous for the trains. Railwaymen working individual points had to know whether approaching trains were stopping or going non-stop through Reading. A mistake on one occasion led to the *Flying Dutchman* express service being directed into the station platform at high speed (fortunately without serious harm being done).

The situation only got more confusing when the railway provided both broad and standard gauge tracks with their own platforms, again on the south side of the tracks. Rather than building four separate ticket offices to serve broad and standard gauge travellers going to or from London, the single yellow-brick and Bath-stone station building (now occupied by a pub) was opened in 1870.

Reading Station today.

Brunel had seen the problems with his one-sided station arrangement and as early as 1853 had submitted plans to change it (which were not accepted). The townspeople had also been lobbying for a better station. They nearly got their wish in 1858, when an unclosed door on a passing goods wagon brought down the pillars supporting part of the old station roof. But the one-sided track layout problem did not get properly sorted out until the wholesale reconstruction of the station in 1896–99, when the station got a new track layout and went from having one very long platform to ten separate ones.

30. Reading Old Cemetery (1842)

In early nineteenth-century Reading, the dead were a severe health hazard to the living. The ancient churchyards were full and, with 600 deaths a year, the authorities had nowhere to bury them. In St Giles' churchyard they buried the dead in the pathways, while in St Mary's gravediggers were reportedly hacking up decomposing corpses to make room for new ones.

The answer came in a private Act of Parliament in 1842, setting up the Reading Cemetery Company. They created a new cemetery site at Hattons Platt, to the east of the built-up area of the town and outside the borough, as it then was. It was one of Victorian England's first garden cemeteries. These were a profit-making commercial proposition, but were also intended to be practical and educational. As a contemporary book on garden cemeteries by landscape architect John Loudon put it, 'They might become a school for instruction in architecture, sculpture, landscape gardening, arboriculture, botany and in those important parts of general gardening, neatness, order and high keeping.'

The landscaping was carefully planned to give aesthetic pleasure while minimising the loss of valuable burial space. The landscaping contract was entrusted to local seedsmen Suttons, and they included a row of specimen trees. The promoters exercised strict control over entry. There was a substantial wall around the cemetery and the classical gateway was there, partly to attract a nicer class of customer, but also to enable them to control who visited the cemetery.

Strict segregation was practised, with separate areas for Anglican and Nonconformist burials, separated by a wall (as if neighbours were likely to trespass on each other). The unconsecrated area devoted to dissenting 'chapel' burials was closer to the cemetery entrance, so that they did not have to pass over the consecrated ground devoted to 'church' burials. Church and chapel even had their own places of worship in the cemetery (now demolished, but designed by different architects – William Brown for the Anglicans and Nathaniel Briant for the Nonconformists).

At first the townspeople were unwilling to use the new graveyard, until the Burial Act of 1852 forced them to stop using the old churchyards. Despite an early twentieth-century extension the cemetery is itself now full up with 18,327 grave plots, but the Grade II-listed cemetery gatehouse is still a landmark in the eastern end of the town.

The Grade II-listed cemetery gatehouse.

The Reading Photographic Establishment.

31. The Reading Photographic Establishment (1843)

The inventor of modern photography, William Henry Fox-Talbot, was Lord of the Manor of Laycock in Wiltshire and MP for Chippenham. After three years of experimenting with his new process, he decided in 1843 to set up an establishment to produce his calotype photographs commercially. He looked for somewhere on the railway line between his home and his business interests in London, and settled on a former school in what was then called Russell Terrace, Reading (now No. 55 Baker Street). There he opened his Reading Photographic Establishment, run for him by a Dutchman, Nicholas Henneman.

In the first seven months alone, the establishment produced some 10,400 prints and an illustrated book, *The Pencil of Nature*. The local outlet for these was Lovejoys stationers in London Street, from where they also bought their supplies of paper. The business was not well received by many locals, who suspected them of being banknote forgers, and they only survived in the town until 1847 when they moved to London. But they left behind a fascinating record of the street scenes in early Victorian Reading, one of the first towns in the world to be so documented.

32. Reading Prison (1844)

There have been several prisons in Reading over the centuries, many of them documented elsewhere in this book – the subterranean cells on Castle Street where St Mary's Church now stands the lock-ups in the former abbey gateway by St Laurence's Church and the derelict remains of Greyfriars Church. By the 1840s the main prison was a building on

The prison today.

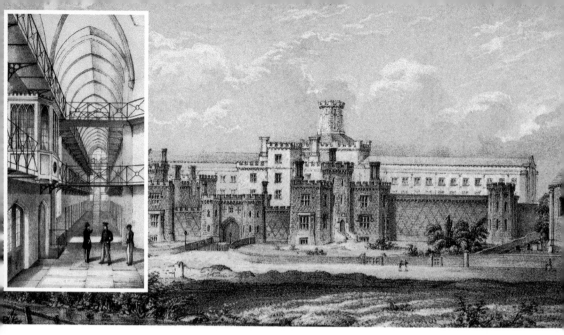

An early depiction of the prison. *Inset*: interior.

the present prison site. Designed in the 1780s by Robert Bressingham, by the 1840s it had proved to be jerry-built and was grossly overcrowded.

In 1842 a competition was launched to design a replacement, based on the New Model Prison at Pentonville. It was won by a partnership headed by one of the most eminent Victorian architects, George Gilbert Scott (whose other works were to include the Home Office, St Pancras station hotel, the Albert Memorial and, locally, the rebuilding of the Reading Abbey Gateway). The Gothic fantasy he produced was said to have been modelled on Warwick Castle, complete with turrets and crenellations. The *Illustrated London News* of the day described it as '... the most conspicuous building and, architecturally, by far the greatest ornament to the town.' Much of this ornament was lost in a brutally functional remodelling in 1971. Inevitably, there was a huge cost overrun on the 1842 project, from the original £15,000 estimate to the final bill of £43,648.

The prison worked on the 'separate' system, in which prisoners were not allowed any communication whatsoever with each other. There were also public hangings, conducted on the flat roof above the gatehouse and drawing crowds of up to 10,000, until public hanging was discontinued nationally in 1868. Reading's last public execution was in 1862.

Many different classes of miscreants served time inside the prison: common criminals, people guilty of breaches of workhouse discipline, young offenders, Irish republicans and, during the wars, offending servicemen or aliens thought to be a security risk. But by far the most famous inmate was Oscar Wilde, who served part of his sentence for 'gross indecency' in Reading, from November 1895. At the time of writing the prison was standing empty, with the government puzzling about what to do with this listed, high-maintenance building.

33. Heelas Department Store, Broad Street (1854)

In 2001 the John Lewis Partnership decided that its Reading store would be rebranded with the Partnership's own name, but for shoppers of a certain age it will forever be known

Above: Heelas Department Store.

Below: Heelas Department Store.

by the name of its founder. John Heelas already had a shop in Wokingham when, in 1854, he decided to open a new store at No. 33 Minster Street with his sons, John and Daniel. They described themselves as 'linen and woollen drapers, silk mercers, etc.' Over the years they acquired neighbouring shops. By 1874 they had a Broad Street frontage and three years later they were describing themselves as a department store. Their departments even included funerals and until well into the twentieth century you could call into the store to buy monumental masonry.

The shop soon established a reputation for excellence. By 1890 they were made by appointment to the Prince of Wales linen drapers and house furnishers, a warrant that continued on his accession to the throne as Edward VII. More recently, in 2007 Elizabeth II awarded them the warrant of suppliers of household and fancy goods. At the other end of the social scale they used to supply uniforms to the prisoners at Reading gaol (17s 10d – 89p – for men, 13s 9d – 69p – for boys). They were even unwitting accomplices to murder. The notorious baby killer, Annie Dyer, bought the tape with which she strangled her infant charges from the store.

The store grew and grew. It became a public company in 1897, and the store was rebuilt in 1907. By the 1950s it was the largest store in Berkshire but still needed further expansion. The rear, the Minster Street part of their site, was eventually demolished and by 1985 had been replaced by a new five-storey building. The store traded continuously throughout the six-year building programme.

Talks about a possible takeover by the John Lewis Partnership began as long ago as 1937, but did not reach a conclusion. In 1947 the store was sold to property tycoon Charles Clore, and three years later to the United Drapery Stores. It was they who sold it to the John Lewis Partnership in 1953.

34. Christ Church, Whitley

Whitley was a Saxon hamlet, built on a small area of cleared land on the edge of the Windsor Forest. The name means 'white clearing', possibly a reference to the local geology. It is called Witelei in the Domesday Book (1086) and in the twelfth century the whole area was given to Reading Abbey. They had considerable landholdings in medieval Whitley, including a manor, a spring that supplied the abbey with water, a village and an extensive park, where the abbot would take his guests hunting. The manor was held by the abbey until the Dissolution and thereafter passed through the hands of many leading Reading families – the Englefields, Knollyses, Vachels, Watlingtons and Kendricks. During the Civil War Harrison's Barn on Whitley Hill was the southern limit of the Royalist defences during the siege of the town and it is thought that the great House at Whitley Park may have been destroyed during those hostilities.

Until the 1860s the area was part of St Giles' parish, when growth in the area led to pressure for a separate church. The church was designed by Henry Woodyer, a disciple of Pugin, best known for his churches in the medieval style. Among his other local works were St Paul's, Wokingham and Clewer Abbey, Windsor. This example of his work is relatively restrained, though it has medieval touches, such as the gargoyles on the tower depicting a monk, a fish, a lion and an eagle.

Christ Church, Whitley.

Construction started in 1861 and the church was consecrated on 7 August 1862. Such was the demand that the church was enlarged in 1874. Schools were also provided and attracted over 400 scholars. Despite Reading's historic lack of burial space the churchyard was never consecrated for burials and is given over to gardens. One missing feature from the gardens is a fifty-foot flagpole, planted there in 1954 but subsequently described as 'lost' (how do you lose a fifty-foot flagpole?).

35. Reading Workhouse, Oxford Road (1864)

Before 1834, care of the poor was based on laws operated by individual parishes and going back to the time of Elizabeth I. Many thought there was a lot wrong with those laws. They discouraged employers from paying a living wage, they did not encourage people to look for work, or to leave the workhouse once they were in it, and they cost the ratepayer too much. In 1834 a new system was introduced. It was much harsher, so that people would only use it if they were desperate, and to do so they had to enter the workhouse and work as hard as the poorest-paid labourer outside the workhouse, but for less. Couples and families were rigidly segregated.

The new system also introduced Poor Law Unions, groups of parishes that were intended to be more efficient than them operating separately. All three Reading parishes were included in one union. At first, the union tried to make do with its pre-1834 accommodation, but with a growing population this was soon grossly overcrowded. In 1864 they finally decided to build a single new workhouse to serve all the union, on a site on the former borough boundary, at Oxford Road.

Battle Hospital, the converted workhouse. *Inset*: formerly named, Reading War Hospital.

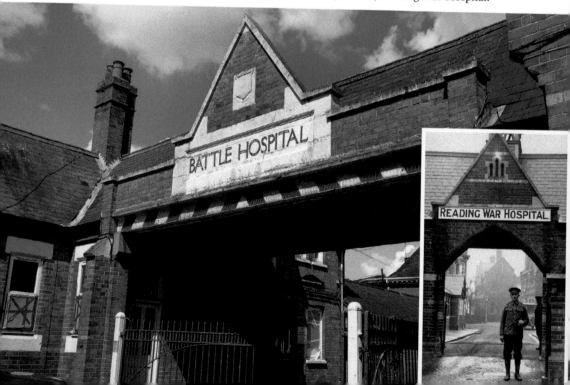

For the next fifty years this workhouse catered – not always very adequately – for the needs of Reading's poor. Being in the workhouse carried a considerable stigma. Women giving birth there used to omit their address from the birth certificate until it was ruled illegal to do so. They then just wrote '344 Oxford Road' with no reference to the institution. The distinctive uniform the inmates were required to wear was a further bone of contention.

Come the First World War and the inmates were moved to other institutions. The workhouse was turned into one of the country's largest hospitals for the war wounded. After the war it continued its hospital-type role, caring for the elderly and infirm, something which it did until 1953. Care of the poor was transferred from the Poor Law Guardians to the local authorities in 1930, at which time the workhouse buildings became known as Battle Hospital. The hospital closed in 2005.

36. Foxhill House, Whiteknights (1868)

The Whiteknights estate has a history going back to Norman times, though there are various theories as to who the original white knight was. One version identifies him as John de Erleigh IV, a descendant of William Marshal, first Earl of Pembroke, who effectively ruled the country as regent during the minority of Henry III. Another has him as Gilbert de Montalieu, the son of a friend of William the Conqueror, who mistakenly slew the brother of the woman he loved. A third links the name to a leper colony that once existed in the area.

The estate was for centuries owned by the De Erleigh and Englefield families. From 1798 it was home to the spendthrift Marquis of Blandford (later to be Duke of Marlborough),

Foxhill House, Whiteknights.

Foxhill.

who bankrupted himself lavishing huge sums of money on his home and the landscaping of its grounds, and on wild entertainments. He moved out in 1819 and his stately home was demolished in 1840. The estate was subdivided into six building plots in 1867. One plot was bought by Alfred Waterhouse, one of Britain's greatest Victorian architects, on which he built a home for himself, Foxhill. He lived there relatively briefly, moving to Yattendon Court in 1877. It was later bought by Rufus Isaacs, who was at different times Reading's MP, Lord Chief Justice of England, British Ambassador to the United States and Viceroy of India.

Isaacs sold the lease in 1919 to Hugo Hirst, founder of the General Electric Company. He and his family lived there until about 1958, when the lease fell in and it became part of the new campus of the University of Reading. The university's growth was being seriously hampered by its constricted site at London Road and a chance dinner, in which the freehold owner of Whiteknights found himself sitting next to the university's bursar, had led to them buying the freehold of the entire estate. After a spell as student accommodation Foxhill was extensively restored in 2003–05 and is now home to the university's School of Law. It is a Grade II-listed building.

37. Jackson's Department Store, Jackson's Corner (1875)

The proprietors of the Broad Street Mall had to resort to special pleading to get the council to rename that part of the Oxford Road adjoining their centre as Broad Street. Another business got a similar result by public acclaim. Edward Jackson opened his first store in September 1875, selling clothing (school uniforms a speciality) and other goods at Market Place, in the premises now occupied by the Oxfam bookshop. The first week's takings were just £92 13s 6d, but it flourished and expanded around the corner, into Kings Road. Not content with that, he set up a hardware store across the road, on the corner of Duke Street and Kings Road.

The whole junction became popularly known by about 1901 as Jackson's Corner and the name was emblazoned in large letters across the front of the store. Further branches followed, at High Street, London Road and Oxford Street, Reading, and in Caversham, Bracknell, Goring-on-Thames, Oxford, Henley, Camberley and Maidenhead. All these other stores had ceased trading by 1994.

When not retailing, Jackson was a councillor and Mayor of Reading (1905–07). He was a firm, paternalistic employer, who would fine his staff for chattering or addressing their colleagues by anything other than their surnames. Four generations of the family ran the store throughout its 138-year history

A feature of the main Reading store was the Lamson system of pneumatic tubes used to transport cash and documents around the building. Installed in the 1940s, by the time the store closed it was the last working example of its kind in the world. The period charm of the store (and the tubes) featured in an episode of the television detective programme *Endeavour*.

Closure of the store came on Christmas Eve 2013 and was attributed to building maintenance costs and competition from the Oracle. Sixty staff lost their jobs. An auction of the shop's internal fittings (again including the pneumatic tube system) raised £75,000, and the town was swept with a wave of nostalgia, with a play, film for a documentary, a museum display and a Facebook group all inspired by the store.

Jackson's Department Store.

38. Shire Hall (1899)

Until 1889 there was a bewildering variety of public bodies delivering services to the community. The 1888 Local Government Act sought to rationalise this and the Berkshire County Council met for the first time on 1 April 1889. Reading was a separate county borough and was administratively not part of Berkshire County Council. So, by basing itself in Reading, the county council for most of its life had headquarters outside its administrative area.

The county council had modest beginnings. Its meetings took place – quarterly – in one of the courtrooms in the assize courts in the Forbury. The only way journalists could cover meetings was by sitting in the dock. A specially adapted courtroom was provided by 1903, and was used for full council meetings until 1980, but it was still cramped. The council's duties were initially not onerous – many of the members held other public offices (they initially included four MPs) and the chief officers managed to fit council duties in around their private practices. Such staff as they employed were housed in three terraced houses next to the assize courts.

This accommodation quickly became inadequate as the council's responsibilities multiplied. An architectural competition was launched to design a new Shire Hall on the site of the three terraced houses. The competition specification was not followed precisely in the final building, due to a combination of penny-pinching and whimsy, like the chairman reducing the size of the office space to give 'wider and more elegant corridors'. The building was occupied in 1911 and almost immediately proved to have

Above: Shire Hall.

Right: Shire Hall.

insufficient space. By the end of the Second World War, council officers were housed in buildings scattered all over Reading.

The first relocation scheme appeared in 1947. The council approved it but not the £260,000 it would cost to build. Ten years later, a scheme to relocate to Maiden Erleigh was also rejected. A 1960s scheme in central Reading fell victim to planning problems and claims of prematurity, with local government reorganisation pending. In 1972 the council bought a redundant RAF station at Shinfield Park. There they built a new Shire Hall costing almost £29 million. The Queen opened it in 1982 but by 1998 the county council itself disappeared in a new round of local government reorganisation. As for the old Shire Hall, it is now an upmarket hotel.

39. McIlroy's Department Store, Oxford Road (1903)

William McIlroy was an Irish draper who came to England and in 1875 opened his first department store in Regent Street, Swindon. The business grew and William's brother-in-law James Wheeler and son Ewart joined the business, one of a chain across England and Wales.

One of the most spectacular of these was the branch at Oxford Road (opposite what is now Broad Street Mall). With its 2,000 square feet of brightly lit plate glass at ground- and first-floor levels, it quickly became known as the Crystal Palace of Reading. As part of its opening publicity a local poet, J. Mosdell wrote the proprietor a fawning letter of

McIlroy's department store. *Inset*: detail of the brickwork.

congratulation and an equally sycophantic twenty-verse poem of praise, which McIlroy promptly had published in its entirety. In a previous publication I could not bring myself to quote more than the opening verse:

> Stupendous building of superb design!
> Unique, original and unsurpassed
> Strength and utility throughout combine
> And in its every single detail shine
> Most beautiful, although so huge and vast.

Those thirsting for more are referred to the *Reading Standard* of 2 January 1904. The store was for many years a key destination for Reading's shoppers, but by the 1950s it struggled to compete; it ceased trading in 1955, to be replaced by one of the first supermarkets.

McIlroys had an unexpected link with music-making in Reading. In March 1944 a meeting was held in the store. Many of those attending had been members of the Berkshire Symphony Orchestra, which had been disbanded when war broke out in 1939. They decided to found the Reading Symphony Orchestra. The new orchestra had two distinguished vice-presidents – the composer Ralph Vaughan Williams and the conductor John Barbirolli. Another keen supporter was their host and the wartime Mayor of Reading, William McIlroy, who had also been a vice-president of the pre-war Berkshire Symphony Orchestra. He also provided the venue for the orchestra's Thursday night rehearsals – the Jacobean Restaurant in the store. No time was wasted, and the orchestra gave its first concert in the town hall in July 1944. The orchestra is still going strong more than seventy years later.

This was not the McIlroy group's only association with music. In the 1930s a grand ballroom was added to their Swindon store, complete with chandeliers and panelling from the cruise liner *Mauritania*. Among the stars to perform there were the Beatles.

40. Caversham Library (1907)

Caversham Library stands as a monument to the extraordinary generosity of one man. Andrew Carnegie (1835–1919) was a Scot who immigrated to the United States. He worked in a number of manual occupations before discovering a genius for steel-making, building a huge steel-making empire which he was able to sell for $480 million in 1901. He then proceeded to give away over $350 million of that money to a host of good causes, arguing that 'the man who dies thus rich dies disgraced'.

Carnegie had little formal education and one of his passions was for libraries. He funded over 2,500 of them worldwide, 300 of which were in Britain. Caversham was one of these, opened in 1907 (Battle Library on Oxford Road was another). It stands on the site of the former Caversham House Academy, on land donated by a local benefactor, Bullivant Williams. It is described as being in the 'Free renaissance' style, or alternatively 'a piece of architectural whimsy'. One piece of whimsy that was not part of the original design was the statue of Father Time. This was added in 1911, at the request of Caversham Urban District Council when they were absorbed into Reading in that year.

Detail on the building.

Caversham Library.

Caversham had had a lending library and reading room since 1883 (on Gosbrook Road, near the Clifton Arms), which was part-funded by the parish council. But it was neither free nor particularly accessible, only opening for book-lending on alternate Wednesdays at midday. Nor was it the local authority, but a voluntary group, that made the bid for Carnegie funding. The council initially opposed it, on the grounds that part of the cost might fall on them. They were only shamed into backing it when Carnegie came up with most of the funds.

The library was opened on 23 March 1907 by Bullivant Williams. He promised to ensure that 'all books of a pernicious nature were kept out of the library'. The library was under-resourced from the start. Lighting was cut down to save money and they relied heavily on donated or second-hand books. There was no phone at first; they used to send semaphore messages from the roof to the central library, which was at that time in line of sight. But the library survived and by 2015 was issuing 163,306 books a year.

41. St Barnabas' Church, Grove Road, Emmer Green (1929)

Reading's churches incorporate some unusual building materials. The tower of St Giles used conglomerate, a local stone consisting of pebbles set in a form of natural concrete; St Mary's Castle Street has a portico made of coadestone, a manufactured form of building material. But first prize must go to the original St Barnabas' Church, consecrated on 17 June 1897 to serve what was then the freestanding hamlet of Emmer Green. It was made of corrugated iron (nicknamed the 'tin tabernacle'), and at that time stood in the middle of open fields a short distance from Emmer Green itself. This was good news for local undertakers. Prior to St Barnabas', a death in Emmer Green could mean a long walk carrying the deceased to St Peter's, Caversham, needing a change of pall-bearers halfway.

The building (costing £410) originally had a spire and neo-Gothic windows. Between 1940 and 1948 it served as two school classrooms, divided by a curtain. It still stands today, newly refurbished and serving as a church hall. A more permanent replacement church costing £2,200 was consecrated on 29 June 1929. St Barnabas has been extended in recent years to provide a parish centre, with offices, meeting rooms and the other requirements of a modern parish.

There was some mystery about the church's organ, which was for some time thought to have come from the grand salon of the stately home at nearby Caversham Park (*see* 2. Caversham Park). But it turns out to have been a new 'off-the-peg' model from an organ builder in Oxford, and was paid for by one John Hill of Caversham Place Park (hence the confusion with Caversham Park). Caversham Place Park was the name of an exclusive residential development, started in 1846 just off the Peppard Road and centred around Grosvenor Road and Derby Road. John Hill lived at Rothesay, Grosvenor Road, certainly between 1901 and 1911.

As for St Barnabas himself, he was a first-century Cypriot-born Apostle, the founder of the Cypriot Church. He travelled with St Paul, before falling out with him and parting company. Apparently not a single word of his is immortalised in the New Testament, but he was known as 'the encourager'.

St Barnabas' Church.

42. Reading Bridge House, George Street (1961)

For as long as the town's waterways were a corridor of communication for local industry, and for many years afterwards, Reading allowed unsightly industrial activity to accumulate along its river and canal banks. It reached the stage where central Reading was possibly the biggest eyesore of any stretch of the Thames. Belatedly, in 1978, the council published a waterways plan for the borough with the aim of reclaiming the town's rivers as an amenity. Over thirty years on, much has been achieved, but much remains still to be done.

One long-established eyesore was the ironworks that stood immediately to the east of Reading Bridge, on the south bank of the Thames, and in 1961 a developer came along with a scheme that (in his view at least) would be a more fitting use of this prominent site. We now know his scheme as Reading Bridge House, the town's first high-rise office building and still a prominent landmark over half a century later. By Reading standards the building has been remarkably long-lived, for many of the office developments that came after it have already been demolished and replaced.

The ten-storey office building was not universally welcomed by the town. There were those who said it would be over-dominant in its location and that it would add to local traffic congestion. Related to this were the perennial concerns about fuelling local labour shortages. On this last point, the developers were apparently able to persuade the powers that be that the office building would employ no more people than the ironworks it replaced. Quite how 113,778 square feet of office floorspace could create no more jobs beggars belief – that ironworks must have been a very crowded place!

Reading Bridge House.

This office building has enjoyed something of a renaissance in recent years. Investors bought it from the receiver in 2013 for £10.85 million, refurbished it and, within a year, sold it on for £35.2 million to the property company that owns the nearby offices at Apex Plaza with the new office development going onto the former Metal Box site. Being just four minutes away from the prestigious new railway station, with electrification and Crossrail in prospect, it could be that Reading Bridge House has a considerable future in prospect.

43. Broad Street Mall (1972)

By the 1950s the pattern of retailing in Reading's town centre was changing. Instead of a row of locally based family businesses supplying a single part of a family's shopping needs, we saw the emergence of all-purpose supermarkets on the American model, and national chains that threatened to leave every town looking just like its neighbours. Another change, waiting in the wings, was the indoor shopping mall.

Indoor shopping was not unknown in Reading. As long ago as the 1890s the Market Arcade provided an under-cover shopping link between Town Hall Square and Broad Street. Most of it was destroyed in the air raid of 1943 but it was rebuilt between 1957 and 1965 as the Bristol and West Arcade. In recent years this has gone downhill to the point of dereliction and plans to redevelop it have so far come to naught. In 1929 businessman John Harris developed the arcade that still bears his name around the junction of Friar Street and Station Road.

Broad Street Mall.

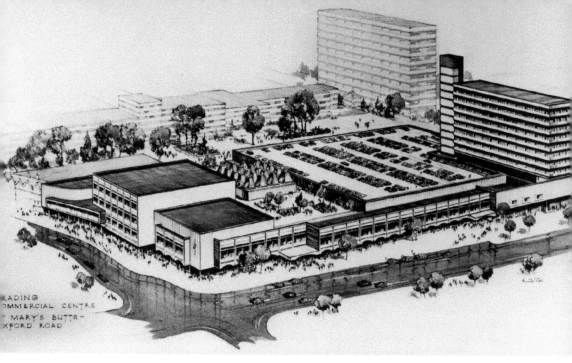

EADING
OMMERCIAL CENTRE
· MARY'S BUTTS —
XFORD ROAD

The Reading Commercial Centre – Reading's first major shopping centre.

But neither of these met the description of a mall on the American lines. The inspiration for one first appeared in 1956, but it took around a decade to identify and assemble a site. This took the form of a comprehensive redevelopment of an area of run-down property that made possible the Civic Centre, the Hexagon and part of the Inner Distribution Road, as well as the shopping centre. The Reading Commercial Centre, as it was originally called, gave the town 400,000 square feet of shopping in 85 shops and 740 car parking spaces, and opened for business in 1972. The architecture was, to put it kindly, of its time. Television magician David Nixon, who opened the centre, said that he had never seen anything like it.

It has had successive upgrades over the years, including two changes of name, becoming in turn the Butts Centre and the Broad Street Mall. But one unexpected transformation came in the form of a retail riot, when the arrival of two Coronation Street stars to open a shop prompted the 4,000 (mostly female) crowd to do extensive damage to the store, to the stars' chauffeur-driven Bentley and to each other (three of the crowd were hospitalised).

44. Civic Offices (1976)

The peripatetic nature of local government over the centuries is documented in the entry for the old Town Hall. But by the start of the twentieth century, with the latest phase of the old Town Hall barely finished, the council was once again short of space. The search for new premises was on again, and this time it took about seventy-five years to resolve.

A host of possible sites were considered, most of them improbable, alarming or both – the Forbury Gardens, London Road, Reading Prison, Hills Meadow and Prospect Park. In the 1957 Development Plan a site north of London Road and west of Princes Street was reserved for a future civic centre, but the idea was fortunately short-lived.

Civic Offices.

Attention then shifted to an area at the western edge of the town centre, where the redevelopment of a run-down area presented an opportunity to meet a number of objectives for the town, including building part of the Inner Distribution Road and a modern covered shopping centre. Sites were also earmarked for a new civic centre, a police headquarters, magistrates' courts and the Hexagon entertainments centre. Demolition began in 1972 and in 1978 the Queen arrived in Reading for the official opening of the new civic centre (in reality it had been occupied some time earlier).

For almost forty years the offices were at the heart of the town's civic life, but by 2012 they had reached the end of their design life. They had asbestos problems and a threat of legionella; the building was high-maintenance and energy inefficient, had inadequate public access and the services were worn out. It needed £100 million spent on it, and a move to alternative premises was a cheaper option.

In late 2014, almost 1,000 staff were relocated to Plaza West on Bridge Street. It was a second-hand building and not purpose-built as a civic centre, but would cost around £60 million over twenty-five years. It should also be 75 per cent more energy efficient and give a better service to the public. Meanwhile the demolition of the old Civic Offices was due to start in January 2016, as this was being written. In the short term it was planned to turn the site into a pocket park, while a developer was found to provide a mixture of housing and shops on the site.

45. The Hexagon, Queens Walk (1977)

In the 1960s lovers of live entertainment in Reading were having a hard time of it. The last purpose-built venue of any size, the Palace Theatre, had been demolished in 1961.

The Hexagon.

The Hexagon.

All that was left was the old Town Hall, whose facilities were far from ideal for either audience or performers, and whose future was itself uncertain. Various ideas, such as a theatre on the university campus, came to nothing, and it seemed that everyone wanted something slightly different. But then, as part of the new Civic Centre complex, the council in 1973 announced plans to build a highly versatile new theatre. The design was entrusted to Johnson-Marshall and Partners, who were designing the Civic Centre next door, and whose other work included the Royal Festival Hall in London.

It was designed to accommodate theatre, conferences and exhibitions and could be switched from a proscenium theatre to a concert hall. It cost £2 million to build and was completed by 1977. Today, the theatre is able to accommodate an audience of 946 for theatre performances, 1,200 for seated concerts and over 1,600 for standing events.

46. Apex Plaza (1989)

Apex Plaza is one of Reading's largest modern office buildings (and certainly one of its pinkest – legend has it that even the architect, on seeing the completed item, reeled back, saying, 'I didn't realise it was going to be *that* pink!'). But for most of the past two centuries the site was the location of central Reading's other main railway station.

This line was originally a branch off the route between London Bridge and Dover, which it joined at Redhill. This railway reached Reading in 1849, stopping at a temporary halt north of Forbury Road before moving to its permanent home (where Apex Plaza now stands) in 1855. A through service to London (initially to London Bridge) was operated

Apex Plaza.

from 1852. The original station was struck by lightning and burnt down in 1859. Its replacement was expanded from two platforms to four in 1896.

Electrification on the Southern Railway (as it was from 1923) started from Waterloo and gradually worked its way outwards. Having reached Wandsworth by 1915, it took until January 1939 to reach Reading.

One of the station's busiest times followed the evacuation from Dunkirk in 1940. Over the course of a few days, 293 special trains arrived in Reading from Dover and the other Channel ports, before being handed over to the Great Western Railway. It was all very ad hoc. Many drivers left the ports without even knowing where they were going. They had no instruction other than to 'stop at Guildford and ask for directions'. Prior to that, one of the town's biggest mass migrations was the 25,000 evacuees that arrived in Reading station, one long weekend in September 1939.

In 1949 the station became known as Reading South, and later Reading Southern (at the same time the Western Region station was renamed Reading General). But soon improvements to Reading General station meant they could now accommodate the Waterloo and Guildford services there, and in September 1965 passenger services from Reading Southern ceased. The station was demolished and used as a car park. But it had one final bonus for transport in Reading. In 1989 the site was sold for the Apex Plaza development, funding a £20 million improvement to the station's ticketing and access facilities.

47. Madejski Stadium (1998)

Reading Football Club has a long and somewhat chequered history. Founded in 1871, they are the oldest club south of the River Trent in the current Football League, which they

Madejski Stadium.

joined in 1920. For most of their existence they played at Elm Park, in its latter years a somewhat dilapidated stadium near the town centre, before moving in 1998 to the £37 million 25,000 seater Madejski Stadium in south Reading. It is named after Sir John Madejski, the club's owner at the time (and abbreviated by the fans to the Mad Stad). The team are nicknamed the Royals, from their association with the royal county of Berkshire (or the Biscuitmen, from Reading's association with Huntley & Palmers).

The Elm Park era saw both triumph (an FA Cup semi-final against Cardiff in 1927 and the winning of the Simod Cup at Wembley against First Division Luton in 1988) and disaster (an 18-0 FA Cup defeat to Preston North End in 1894, thought to be the biggest margin of defeat of any club still in the Football League). But the Madejski era can already match those triumphs, with two (admittedly brief) spells in the top Premier League and a closely contested FA Cup semi-final against Arsenal in 2015.

48. The Oracle (1999)

A Reading man, John Kendrick, made his fortune as a clothing manufacturer in London. When he died in 1624 he left the Corporation £7,500 to build a workhouse in which local unemployed people could make a living manufacturing clothing. The Corporation called it the Oracle and it was built on the north bank of the River Kennet. After a long and somewhat chequered history, marked by mismanagement on the part of the Corporation, it was demolished in around 1850.

Much of the area alongside that part of the Kennet was subsequently occupied by the Simonds (later Courage) brewery, and when the brewery moved out to the edge of town in

The Oracle.

The Oracle.

1980 an opportunity for redeveloping a large (14 acre-) part of the town centre arose. At about the same time, town centre shopping was under threat from an out-of-town shopping development to the south of Reading, though (fortunately for Reading) this development never materialised.

Initially the developers were only interested in office development, but the market moved on and, by 1990, the latest planning application was mainly for shopping and leisure. It took twelve years and £250 million to make the redevelopment a reality. It opened in September 1999, increasing the town's shopping floor space by a third and for a time propelling the town into the top ten shopping destinations in the United Kingdom. The site of the centre included that of John Kendrick's former workhouse and the name 'Oracle' was also inherited by the new complex.

The public responded enthusiastically. Over 100,000 of them visited the Oracle on its opening day and 420,000 over the first weekend. Shops reported record sales, some ran out of stock or had to bring in additional staff. Almost two decades later, the crowds in the malls and the queues for the car parks testify to the continuing success of the Oracle.

49. The New Reading Railway Station (2014)

The current modernisation of the station has its origins way back in British Railway's 1955 Modernisation Plan. Building works were planned for 1962 but were never started. A £20-million station concourse was opened in 1989. This gave better ticketing and platform access, but left unsolved the track layout that made Reading Station one of the biggest bottlenecks in the entire network.

By 2014 Reading was the ninth busiest station in the UK outside London and was second only to Birmingham New Street as an interchange station (again outside London); 16.3 million passengers passed through the station in 2014/15. However, before the redevelopment the station had eight terminal platforms and just four through-platforms. This meant that the capacity of the tracks on either side of the station was roughly three times that of the station.

The issue was forced when the area's signalling needed renewing. Could they afford to freeze the old unsatisfactory layout in place for another generation? Instead, the railway embarked on a wholesale redevelopment of the station and the surrounding track, costing (at latest estimate) £895 million, which was nearing completion at time of writing. The new station has five additional new platforms, including four new through-platforms, and is expected to be able to accommodate a 103 per cent increase in capacity by 2035.

To the west of the station a new viaduct (apparently the longest concrete viaduct in the United Kingdom, no less!) carries all the express services over freight and relief lines, and there are even road improvements, with the rail bridges over Cow Lane being widened to give two-way traffic and a cycle path. All of this was officially opened by the Queen in July 2014.

More change is on the way, with electrification being introduced – eventually. It was due to be completed to Bristol by 2016 and Cardiff by 2018. But in late 2015 delays of up to two years and a tripling of the 2013 cost estimate of £874 million were being forecast. Crossrail services into central London from Reading are due to start in December 2019, though journey times from Reading are not expected to be reduced by it.

Reading's new railway station.

50. A Historical Pub Crawl

I am going to cheat a little here and include several town-centre drinking places under a single entry.

50a. *The Allied Arms, St Mary's Butts*

From the front this looks like an eighteenth-century building but, behind the street frontage façade, the overhanging upper storey gives away its sixteenth-century origins. Its out-buildings are said to include part of the site of a former nunnery, including a well. It only seems to have been a pub since 1828, but between 1878 and 1890 it had its own brewery (stout a speciality). The Allies in its name were the Crimean ones – England, France and Turkey. But when Turkey changed sides in a subsequent conflict their flag was painted out. There is a story that in the 1960s, the bar was full of a gang of Irish road workers, thirsty from building the M4, when the then landlord made the mistake of calling time two minutes early. A riot ensued.

The Allied Arms, St Mary's Butts.

5cb. The Alehouse, Broad Street

This may be a relatively new name to Reading drinkers but the premises predate that part of Broad Street. It was known as the Cock Inn in 1565, when Broad Street east was still divided into Fishe Strete and Buchers Rowe. It may look newer than that, but the frontage had to be rebuilt in 1901, when the old one collapsed.

The Alehouse, Broad Street.

The Great Western Hotel (now the Malmaison Hotel).

50c. The Great Western Hotel (now the Malmaison Hotel)

Located opposite the railway station, this lays claims to being designed by Isambard Kingdom Brunel, and to being the oldest railway hotel in the world. Both claims are challenged. But it has had some important visitors over the years. The brother of the then Tsar of Russia and his entourage dined there in 1860. In 1945 Winston Churchill and Anthony Eden took tea there, on their way back from the Yalta conference, where the shape of the post-war world had been agreed between the allied powers.

50d. Fox and Hounds

But, for real celebrity, how about the Fox and Hounds, Gosbrook Road, Caversham? In 1960 the licensees were Mike and Bett Robbins. Bett agreed to let her cousin perform in the pub in return for him working behind the bar. For good measure the cousin, a lad named Paul McCartney, brought his friend John Lennon along to perform with him – whatever became of them?

Fox and Hounds.

Acknowledgements

The historic photographs used in this book are from the collection held by Reading Libraries, and I am grateful to Anne Smith and Katie Amos for their help with these. Thanks also go to Cheryl Dibden and her colleagues for their permission for me to photograph the interior of the former Broad Street Chapel and to my son Michael for many of the modern photographs. I would also like to give general thanks to all those who have taken the time and trouble to document different aspects of the town's history over the years. Lack of space prevents me providing a bibliography or a detailed index. But those wishing to follow up anything covered in this book need look no further than the shelves of the local studies section of Reading Central Library, or the internet.

About the Author

Stuart Hylton has lived and worked in Reading for over thirty-five years. He is the author of some twenty-five books on historical subjects, both local and national. His eldest son, Michael, took many of the modern photographs that illustrate this book.